THIS NOTEBOOK BELONGS TO :

If you find this book anywhere, **please return** it to the address above.

Date : ....

8

Date :

Date : ....

Date : ....

Date : ....

25

Date : ....

Date : ....

Date : ....

Date : ....

Date : ....

Date : ....

Date : ....

Date : ....

Date : ....

Date : ....

Date : ....

Date : ....

Date : ....

Date : ....

Made in the USA
Monee, IL
14 February 2020

21791460R00061